And That Was That

an
abortion memoir

And That Was That

an
abortion memoir

by
Bonnie Brady

world split open press

Joshua Tree, California

Some names and identifying details have been changed to protect the privacy of individuals.

Grateful acknowledgement is made to *Cholla Needles* for publishing a story excerpted from this manuscript, "On The Sparrow," in Issue #33: Survival.

Printed in the United States of America.

ISBN: 978-0-578-80677-8

For the women who didn't make it.

Why Am I Telling You This?

I am an old woman in my 80th year. My baby-making days are far in the past. My experiences as a sexually active and alarmingly fertile young woman ran the gamut, from illegal abortion (a felony in the 1950s and 1960s), to early legalized abortion in my home state of California, with quite a few hoops to jump through, and finally, easy and accessible experiences at women-run clinics, post Roe v. Wade.

In 1964, six months pregnant with my first son (a very much wanted child by both my husband and myself), I was an active board member of the Long Beach YWCA, or Young Women's Christian Association. That socially progressive women's organization was on the forefront of the growing movement to legalize abortion in California. We organized pro-choice workshops with doctors, social workers, and progressive clergy who supported a woman's right to choose. We lobbied, we wrote letters, we made phone calls to our state legislators. We educated each other.

In 1969, the California Supreme Court ruled in favor of a woman's right to abortion in some circumstances. The floodgates opened and pregnant women and girls from all over the country came to California for safe and legal abortions. In 1973, Roe v. Wade was affirmed by the United States Supreme Court. For almost 50 years, American women have had the right to choose safe and legal abortion as an alternative to an unwanted pregnancy.

1

But Roe v. Wade has been under almost constant attack ever since. A mostly old, white, male Congress made sure abortions could not be funded through public health programs. Women approaching clinics are accosted by demonstrators with unpleasant photographs of aborted late-term fetuses, guilt-producing chants of "don't kill your baby", and loudly praying circles of zealots. Private pregnancy clinics opened by fundamentalist churches lure young women with promises of free services and then pressure them to "choose life". Doctors and others providing abortion services face death threats, resulting in both attempted and successful murders of several physicians.

I am alarmed by what I see happening now— funding denied, clinics closed, more lives threatened. There is ramped-up harassment of women entering clinics, most often for health services not related to abortion, such as cancer screening, STD treatment, and birth control services. We've seen severe restrictions placed on women's health providers, to the point that some states have only one clinic in the whole state remaining open. Many states have enacted restrictions based on gestational age. Women of child-bearing age now face the very real threat of losing one of their most important civil rights. This, while Americans overwhelmingly support a woman's right to choose whether or not to carry a pregnancy to term.

There's a meme on Facebook that shows an older woman carrying a sign at a protest march that says, "I can't believe I have to fight this shit all over again." That could be me and that could be my sign.

To today's younger women who have always had the right to choose, and mothers of those who may someday need to make that choice, I give you my experiences. I urge you to remain vigilant, as anti-choice lawmakers determine whether or not you have the right to make decisions about your own bodies. Please don't take your rights for granted.

Believe me, you don't want to go back.

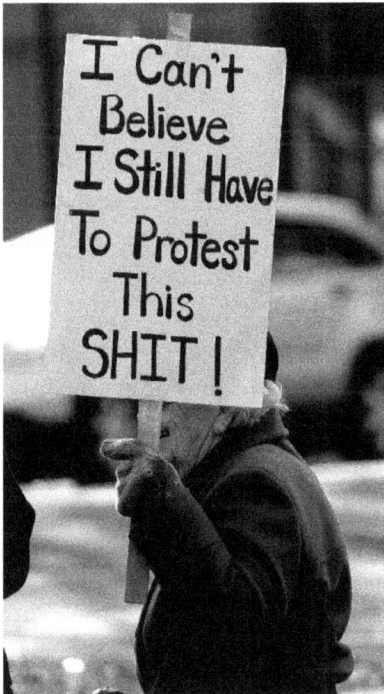

photo credit: Lorraine_M / Shutterstock.com

Knocked Up

If Mother Nature had her way with me, I would have birthed eight children, four of them within the sanctity of marriage, pretty much what I had dreamed of as a young girl. But unplanned pregnancies and fatherless children would have veered my life in a much different direction.

Was I a slut? Of course I was. I didn't start out that way. I was a nice young girl in the 1950s when nice young girls just didn't go "all the way". And those who did usually disappeared from high school in their junior year to go spend several months with an aunt in Minnesota or entered the Florence Crittenton home for unwed mothers.

For many of us "nice" middle class girls who didn't go all the way and had serious boyfriends, the result was we just got married way too young. As soon as we turned 18, or graduated from high school, or dropped out of college after one or two years, we got the white-dress wedding as "technical" virgins, the holy-of-holies hymen intact. That spot of blood on the sheets. The 19-year-old husband who "popped our cherry".

So, my too-early marriage at age 18 to Rick occurred during the summer between my freshman and sophomore years of college. It began to crumble within a year. Our summer job money ran out, and I had to drop out of my sophomore year and get a job. My young husband was focused on his athletic career so wouldn't get even part-time work. And we started having fights that included physical abuse. We separated for a few weeks, but at the urging of his very Catholic parents, we got back together. The reunion resulted in a diaphragm failure and an unintended conception. It also resulted in the realization that it was "over," after the worst fight yet, me walking out, and my husband trying to run me down with his car in the alley behind our apartment.

I went back home and reenrolled in college, and several weeks later realized I had missed my period and had a bout or two of nausea. The divorce papers had been filed and there was no way I was going back to him. I was 19, and the idea of being a single mother was unacceptable to me. At that time, motherhood without accompanying fatherhood was cause for shame, unlike now, where it is one of choices many women make and is well-accepted.

It was 1960 and abortion was illegal. In fact, in the United States it was a felony. My take-charge mother (bless her heart) took charge and asked around. She found a very kind doctor with a clinic in East L.A. who was willing to do a D&C (Dilation and Curettage). I was prepped and given a short-acting sedative, woke up about 15 or 20 minutes later and was told I could expect to bleed for a couple of days, but to let him know if I had any concerns. Aside from some paranoia going to and coming from the clinic, there were no adverse effects. I was back in class in a few days.

And that was that.

~

Back at school, I took up my sophomore year as a biology major, settled into my classes and made some friends. We hung out in the campus coffee shop between classes, and most weekends went out as a group to one of the local jazz clubs. Eventually one of the guys, Henry, and I began dating. I spent time at his apartment, which he shared with his brother, and yes, his mother. We listened to a lot of music and studied together for biology exams, and occasionally we'd sneak off to an upstairs bedroom.

I was horrified at how easy it was to get pregnant. There I was, right on Mother Nature's schedule, pregnant again two years later. Henry was equally horrified. He was a junior on an ROTC scholarship and committed to four years of military service after graduation. Marriage to me was not on his agenda. I was equally uninterested in marriage as an option. I wanted to continue my studies and finish college. And we weren't in love. We were "friends with benefits" before that was a thing. And it was still the early 1960s and abortion was still illegal.

This time, the doctor who had treated me two years earlier was no longer available, and the search for a local alternative was unsuccessful. My mother's housekeeper was from Tijuana and had family there. It was generally known that abortion was available (though also illegal) in Mexico, so my mom asked Tina if she had any recommendations. She called her sister in Tijuana and got the name of a "real" doctor and we got a price and an appointment.

So, my brave mother, $400 cash in hand and a trembling and terrified 21-year-old in the passenger seat, drove us to Tijuana and somehow found that doctor's office. My mom was a proud woman, and as was the custom at the time, we "dressed up" for important appointments. There we were, two affluent looking *gringas* walking into a storefront clinic.

The doctor took one look at us and immediately the price doubled to $800. Mom had only $400 in hand. After some negotiation, the doctor insisted she drive back across the border to a San Diego bank (this was before ATMs) and come back with the additional $400 cash. He told her to leave me there and he would get started. Back then, crossing the border was not the hours long ordeal it is now. Back and forth might take an hour, not much more.

So, off went my mom, and the doctor escorted me out the back door of the clinic to what I recollect was sort of an enclosed, covered patio. I disrobed from the waist down, got up on an exam table and put my feet in the stirrups. As the doctor began shaving my pubic hair, he also instructed me on what to say if the Federales stopped us on the way out of town. He instructed me to tell them nothing, unless they examined me and discovered I was shaved. I guess that was evidence of having had an abortion.

The gist of it was that I was to tell them a nurse had done it on the U.S. side of the border. After prepping me, he gave me a local anesthetic, but no sedation, as had been my previous experience. I was terrified but resigned. Again, the procedure used was a D&C. Vacuum aspiration was newly available in Europe, but not yet available in the U.S. As the procedure progressed, I didn't have much pain, just some pressure and a little discomfort, as my uterus was being scraped clean. I was wide awake, and my main memory of the procedure was the sound—the splat and splash of the contents of my womb into a metal bucket on the floor below my spread legs. As he continued the curettage, he grilled me on what I was to do if we were stopped by the police. I just wanted to close my eyes, turn my head, and grit my teeth, but he insisted I repeat over and over again how I would respond to police questioning. When the procedure was completed, he gave me an antibiotic injection and some pills for later, and I got dressed.

About then, my mother showed up, worried sick, of course, but with the required additional cash. The doctor repeated the instructions for dealing with the police if we were stopped. As far as the procedure was concerned, he reassured my mom that I would be fine.

We fled, made a beeline for the border crossing as I told mom what it had been like. The concern had been so focused on what to do if stopped by the police, we worried that we might have been observed and would end up in the Tijuana jail without any money to get ourselves out. As we crossed back over the border, we heaved a collective sigh of relief. My health was not affected, and we never spoke of the ordeal again. And that was that.

Love and Marriage

After graduating from college with a degree in Biology, I had the summer off and was looking for my first "real" full-time job. I found the ideal position quickly and was scheduled to begin work the first of September.

My summer was lazy, with lots of beach time, and I ran into Jay, an old friend of my ex-husband's, a local lifeguard and soon-to-be high school teacher. We started dating, and in about six months became engaged. We planned for a June wedding, but I came up pregnant in January, so we got our families together and hastily put together a small but joyful wedding.

We moved into a one-bedroom cottage in a Southern California beach town and I enjoyed a healthy pregnancy. I continued to work until two weeks before the birth of our beautiful baby boy in August. We named him William Edward after both grandfathers. I stayed home with the baby and enjoyed beginning the family life I had envisioned for myself. My husband spent that year getting his teaching credential and worked as a lifeguard during the summer, as he had since high school. He had already obtained a teaching and coaching job at the local high school to start in September.

My life seemed quite ideal and I really took to the traditional role of wife and mother. We moved from the tiny beach cottage to a larger, two-bedroom, two story house a block away. It faced the ocean and had a decent sized backyard. Both were rental properties owned by my parents. The yard was nothing but sand, but I started a garden and soon had blossoming flowers and even a few small trees. It was a few weeks before the baby's first birthday, and I was planning a garden party for family.

One idyllic summer afternoon, while my husband was at his lifeguard job, the baby was napping in his upstairs bedroom. I stepped out the front door and walked a short distance up the street to a friend's house to see if she wanted to come for coffee.

I want to explain how close together the houses were. Beach houses were built packed together as close as they could squeeze them in, at most six feet between houses. So "three doors down" wasn't equivalent to the distance in a typical tract neighborhood with spacious lots. Most of these beach cottages were built in the 1930s and 40s with natural wood shingles and roofs.

I knocked on my friend's door, but she wasn't home, so I walked the short distance back. I was gone for no more than three or four minutes.

I opened my front door, and to my horror, the entire, narrow stairwell was fully involved in flames. I ran in but was beaten back by the heat and smoke. There was no possible way to get up the stairs.

I ran back out into the street, screaming for help. At that point, smoke was pouring out of the upstairs. As I thought could only happen on a California beach in July, a vacationing fireman came running up to me from the sand, in his bathing suit. I hysterically babbled something about my baby being in the upstairs bedroom, which had a small balcony facing the street. The fireman bravely tried to get up on the balcony, but was beaten back as well, facing the fire and heat with bare skin.

In total fight or flight panic, I turned and ran out onto the beach to the lifeguard on foot patrol. I screamed at him to call headquarters and get my husband, who was on Jeep patrol somewhere along the ten mile stretch of beach. I turned back to the house and fell to my knees in the sand. The house was fully involved in flame and there was no hope of rescuing the baby. I was devastated, sick. My world slowed to a stop.

The scene around me became surreal, as I watched neighbors on either side running in and out of their houses, now starting to smolder. They ran out with "valuables"—golf clubs, surfboards, silver tea services, trophies, and the like. One neighbor was a famous teen-aged surfing champion. His mother was trying to save his surfing trophies before their house joined the conflagration. An understandable response, I suppose, but my loss was so overwhelming I found her actions profoundly unimportant.

Fire trucks showed up and water was applied to a now total loss. My husband was brought to the scene by his lieutenant. All I could sob was, "He's gone, he's gone". A neighbor took me into their house as the firemen did their work and gave me a glass of scotch to "calm me down".

11

When the fire was extinguished, they began sifting through for the baby's remains, asking me to point out where the crib had been located. My only consolation was that he had been asleep. I was later told cause of death was from smoke inhalation. He was undoubtedly dead before the flames got to him.

My doctor, the same one who had delivered my baby less than a year earlier, made an emergency house call. He gave me an injection of a mild sedative.

There was a picture in the L.A. Times the next morning. The crestfallen vacationing fireman in his bathing suit stood with the smoldering ruins of our house in the background.

My parents, who owned the house, were devastated. They lost their first grandchild. My husband's sister and brother-in-law (coincidentally, a fireman) showed up somehow and took us to my mother-in-law's home nearby. I collapsed into bed with only the clothes on my back, a yellow seersucker sunsuit. Friends and family gathered essentials for the next few days—clothing, shoes, toothbrush, hairbrush, make-up, and a black dress.

We made funeral plans, chose a tiny casket, chose yellow roses with blue ribbon for the floral piece, chose a song, "His Eye Is On The Sparrow". The funeral was held at the church where we were married and the baby had been baptized a few months earlier. I wavered between distraught and numb. We buried the tiny coffin in the children's section of a cemetery in Long Beach. His paternal great-grandparents are nearby.

My world was empty. A baby fills every moment. I no longer had a job. I filled the time replacing material possessions, clothes, dishes, household items. I went through the motions of living on. One of my husband's organizations had collected basic furnishings for our apartment. His junior lifeguards went door to door collecting hundreds of Blue Chip and Green Stamp books for us to replace household items at the catalog stores. They sent sweet notes and cards. Hearts went out to us.

But to tell the truth, I don't remember much about how—or if—my husband and I processed the loss together. I don't remember conversations or crying in each other's arms. I remember frequently crying alone in the bathroom. I remember being told by others that I was "taking it well", which I came to believe meant "don't make me uncomfortable with your grief".

Months later, we purchased a nice tract house with help from my parents. I busied myself decorating, settling in, and becoming more active in a couple of auxiliaries to my husband's clubs. I had no interest in going back to work. I wanted only to get pregnant and continue raising a family. I cooked, crafted, gardened, sewed my own clothes, and kept busy socially. After some months of trying to get pregnant, increasingly frustrated every time my period started, I began using methods of the time (kind of the opposite of the rhythm method), primarily temperature taking and counting days. Love making became baby making and was strictly scheduled and consistently failed to result in a pregnancy—a weird experience for me.

Every month was a heartbreaking disappointment, and I got more and more advice from mother and lady friends saying I was trying too hard and to just relax, and suggestions that I go back to work. One of my husband's friends was working for a new federal "War on Poverty" program, providing activities and enrichment for teenagers living in disadvantaged neighborhoods and public housing projects. I was an assistant program director, teaching crafts and working with the girls who came to the center. The job was a good fit. It was fun, rewarding, and the kids loved me, and I them.

Lo and behold, as I became less focused on getting pregnant, I got pregnant! I continued to work for several months, and then stayed home to "feather my nest" as my due date drew
near. I decorated the heck out of the nursery, in neutral colors as the sonogram was not yet available to reveal the baby's sex.

Again, I had a healthy, uneventful pregnancy, and a few days before my 26th birthday, I went into labor. My son was healthy and adorable, and friends and family were overjoyed for us. I spent the summer of 1967 like any new mother: breastfeeding, washing diapers, calming a crying baby, encouraging first smiles and giggles, always trying to get enough sleep. Trying to take care of myself was challenging.

My husband was minimally helpful and needed a certain amount of care himself—to be fed, to have his clothes and house cleaned, but surprisingly, not to have his sexual needs met, after three months of abstinence. As was the practice at the time, new mothers were to refrain from intercourse for six weeks before birth and six weeks after, then go to the doctor for a final postpartum checkup, get fit for a new diaphragm, and go home, finally able to make love. I was surprised to find my eager availability of no interest.

The weeks and months dragged on with one lame excuse after another as to why lovemaking was of little interest. My self-esteem was eroding day by day. Eventually we began making love occasionally. Around my son's first birthday, thinking another child would be nice, I stopped using birth control and thought I'd just let Mother Nature take her course. Within a few months, I missed my period and felt sure I was pregnant. I told my husband, who seemed happy about it, and my mother, who was delighted. Six weeks later I began bleeding. I went to my doctor. I had not yet had a pregnancy test, and he asked me to bring in the evidence, a slightly clotty menstrual pad. He determined I had miscarried the pregnancy. I was disappointed, but not heartbroken. I assumed I could try again in a few months.

That time, Mother Nature was watching out for me. My body knew what my head and heart had not yet figured out. Several months later, I found out my husband had been having an affair for quite some time, and he left us soon after. My humiliation was complete.

On My Own Again

A year later, I was divorced, working full time at an office job, and my son was in pre-school. My recently ex-boyfriend had a vasectomy, so I had gotten used to not having to worry about getting pregnant. In addition, I had just recovered from hepatitis and the birth control pill was not recommended for me.

I met a cute serviceman at a party—Phil was a little mysterious, I thought. Later, it turned out he was just weird. It was 1970, the sexual revolution was in full swing, and we took full advantage of it. I was a little lax in the "using protection" department, and he was always too stoned to care. He stayed at my apartment for a couple of weeks. I thought he was on leave, turned out he was AWOL. The last straw, as I started my hectic morning routine, getting ready for work and feeding and dressing my kid, was when I came into the living room and there he was, buck naked, standing on his head in the middle of the room, not a care in the world. That evening, after work, I drove him back to Long Beach and dropped him off at the base.

Well, Mother Nature, being her capricious self, decided it was time. The next month I got concerned when my cycle was a little late in cycling. I waited another couple of weeks and when nothing happened, I sought out a newly legal abortion service, advertised in the Los Angeles Free Press. In 1969 the California Supreme Court had ruled in favor of a woman's right to abortion. It was legal, but it was not easy.

First of all, I had to go to an orientation in a large L.A. hotel conference room. I was amazed to join a roomful of young women, some with their mothers. Many of them had been brought to California on a charter flight from Texas, where abortion was still illegal. Roe v. Wade had not yet been decided. We were told about the process, which involved being interviewed by either a psychiatrist or a pastor there at the hotel. They would determine from that 15-minute interview if we were sufficiently at physical risk or emotionally distraught enough to warrant an abortion, thereby preventing an unintended pregnancy from pushing us off our rockers altogether.

I was interviewed by a very kindly mainline protestant minister. Quite rationally, I told him of my single motherhood, low paying 9 to 5 job, somewhat difficult three-year-old who required most of my energy, and complete inability to handle any more than was already on my plate. With a wink and a nod, I was certified "at risk". The next step in the process was to be assigned to one of the participating hospitals to show up to at seven o'clock the next morning and pay the bill. I believe it was $300—for me, that was a month's take home pay.

Since I was not staying at the hotel with the out-of-towners, I was not eligible to be transported on the charter bus. So I was given the address of a small private hospital in South Central L.A. In the morning, my sister picked up my son for the day, and I drove myself to the hospital.

There was a lobby full of about 18 to 20 anxious young women. We changed into hospital gowns and climbed aboard a train of gurneys lined up down the hall outside the operating room. As I got closer to the swinging door of the O.R., a nurse anesthetist gave me an injection of, I believe, Scopolamine, and I pretty much enjoyed a hallucination that can best be described as like "It's a Small World" at Disneyland. When I came out of it, the procedure was over. I got dressed and drove home.

And that was that!

Well, not quite. I had neglected to call in to the office and play sick. I showed up for work the next day and mumbled I hadn't been feeling well. My excuse was full of holes and everyone knew it, but no one ever found out where I had really been. At least I had not been breaking the law.

~

Poor Randy: a sweet, young graduate student with an Old English Sheepdog named Robespierre and an MG convertible. Living the good life in L.A. in the 70s. Then he met me. I was still working the same dead-end but secure office job, my son was now in kindergarten, and I guess I had moved from desperation to hopelessness. I plugged away day by day, with no idea how to change the trajectory of my life.

Randy and I were dating, but for some reason, I just kind of resented him. He was too nice, too young, too not my rescuer.

About then I decided to take a vocational aptitude exam and applied to two graduate programs: Occupational Therapy at USC, and

Anthropology at University of New Mexico. I aced the GRE and was accepted to both programs. My heart wanted to go to New Mexico; my head wanted to stay close to home. My head won.

I was at a crossroads once again, and Mother Nature once again tried to play the biological imperative card. Poor hapless Randy couldn't have been more empathetic, and even helped a little financially.

My health provider of choice was one of the new women's health centers in L.A. Not a commercial venture, but a true health service provider.

I walked into a modest but cozy, homelike lobby and was seen promptly by a counselor. She asked if I would be willing to allow several women being trained to be support volunteers to observe my exam. They looked at my pregnant cervix through the speculum and I was declared about eight weeks pregnant. Not surprised, at about two weeks my breasts were swollen and tender—my first symptom, even before I missed my period.

I proceeded, with my supportive counselor at my side, to the treatment room, assumed the position and the female doctor came in. In the women's clinics the vacuum aspiration procedure had replaced the D&C. No sedation needed, just a local anesthetic to the cervix. My counselor held my hand, reassured me, and explained what was happening each step of the way. There was little discomfort, and again, my main memory is the sound of the small vacuum motor and aspiration.

What a difference from my previous experiences. No terror, no judgement, no guilt trip. The women's clinics brought compassion and true understanding to the experience, as well as a much simpler and safer medical treatment.

Also, the "pro-life" movement had not yet begun their reign of terror at the clinics. No yelling, praying, dead fetus signs waving or threats of everlasting damnation at the doorway. Just a cadre of supportive, compassionate women who truly understood the dilemma of unwanted pregnancy and the rights of women to control their own bodies.

The doctor gave me a prescription for birth control pills before I left the clinic. I rested in the lobby for a while to make sure there was no excessive bleeding, and paid the bill, just $150. I thanked them profusely as I left and made it right on time for my therapy appointment.

And that was that.

~

In the summer of 1973, I entered a two-year Master's program in Occupational Therapy, a field that was in the top three recommendations of the vocational aptitude test I had taken. It was a challenge to balance the care of my son and my full-time program, but I really enjoyed being back in school, and my classmates were a diverse and close-knit group.

During that first year of grad school I spent most weekends at my family's cabin near Mountain Center, studying, unwinding, and spending quality time with my son.

I met Ben, a lumberjack of a man, built like a tank, with missing front teeth, who cut and sold firewood for a living. My son loved watching him fell dead trees out in the forest, and he treated me well enough. At times he worked under the table as a bouncer at a local bar & restaurant. It was then I began to see his violent side, not directed at me, but nonetheless it raised my hackles.

Toward the end of the first year of my graduate program, I had the option of taking my O.T. exam and a B.S. in O.T. or continuing with the additional year for my Master's. Either way, I would be qualified to get a job as a registered O.T.

I had begun to pull away from the relationship, spending less time in the mountains, taking more seriously his reputation as a dangerous guy. The last time I stayed at his place, I was making the bed and found a pair of little girl's panties lost in the bedclothes. I was horrified at the implication and never went back.

Mother Nature stepped right up, and it turned out I got pregnant on that last night, in spite of being on the birth control pill. Back then there were no home pregnancy tests that showed very early if you were or weren't. There was no Plan B morning-after pill, which you can take for three days after unprotected sex to derail any get-together of sperm and ovum. I knew within a few weeks and went back to the women's clinic and had what was termed a "preemptive" abortion, before a pregnancy test would come up positive.

I decided to continue my second year of grad school. And that was that.

~

A year later, I got my first O.T. job near enough to the mountain cabin that I could live there. I spent the summer moving in and getting my son enrolled in school. I saw the lumberjack a few times in town without incident, and assumed he had moved on, as I had. I was getting oriented to my new job and enjoying my new colleagues. Things were going well.

One evening after work, the phone rang. The familiar, gruff voice on the line was Ben. He sounded friendly enough and told me there was a really good band playing at the bar that he thought I'd enjoy. My son was at a sleepaway camp, so I went. It seemed like a chance to get out for a while. When I got to the bar, there were several friends there. I sat with them and ordered a Tequila Sunrise. The band was finishing up its first set when the waitress set a second drink in front of me. She said it was from Ben, sitting at his usual place at the bar when he was working as the bouncer.

I got up, drink in hand, and went over to him. I thanked him but said I didn't want to drink anymore as I had to get up early for work the next morning. I left the drink on the bar and turned to go back to my table, and all hell broke loose! Yelling obscenities, he grabbed me around the waist and dragged me across the room toward the door. I grabbed ahold of a post in the entry but had no chance to pull away. He was fury unleashed. As we hit the door, he gave me a shove, and down the three steps I went, landing hard. With a sharp pain and audible snap, I knew my lower leg was fractured.

As he came at me, I sat up and pulled up my pant leg. My lower leg and ankle were jutting off at a stomach-turning angle. He stopped in his tracks, yelling, "Get up, get up!" I screamed at him, "You broke my leg! Go call an ambulance." He complied, thank goodness.

As I lay there in excruciating pain, waiting for the EMTs, I saw people inside timidly looking out the window, or huddled at the door. Nobody came to my assistance. They were all too afraid of Ben's wrath.

The ambulance arrived relatively quickly and transported me to the local hospital. They sent me on to a larger hospital with orthopedics specialists. My injury required four hours of surgery, numerous metal objects to hold it all back together, ten days in the hospital, and three months on crutches in a hip-to-toe cast.

A month later, after recuperating enough to return to work and learning to drive with my right leg in a cast, I went back to my cabin and got my son enrolled in school. I thought everything would be okay. I thought he had learned his lesson.

Well, I was wrong. He began stalking me and I became more and more concerned. One evening, after getting home from work, I had an overwhelming feeling of dread. My intuition was telling me loud and clear to get out of there. I grabbed a few necessities, put my son in the car, and took off. We disappeared from our little cabin in the mountains.

Later, I heard through the grapevine that he had been looking for me with a gun that night, because he had been in court on assault and battery charges my lawyer insisted I file. He was found guilty and fined $100.

I had retained a lawyer while in the hospital, and he sent an investigator to the bar to get their side of the story. One of the owners let it slip that Ben had actually planned to rape me that night.

I never saw him again, but for years afterward, whenever I saw a man in a black knit watch cap, I suffered panic attacks. For several years I lived with major anxiety.

So, why am I telling this unfortunate story as part of my saga of abortion experiences? Because if I'd had Ben's child, I would have been tied to him. If I'd had to depend on the legal system at the time to protect me, I might not have survived. There literally was no domestic abuse protection for women at that time. No shelters, little or no law enforcement training or sense of urgency. Most women were on their own when it came to escaping their abusers. My solution was to simply "disappear". That would have been much more difficult or impossible if I had his child.

So I am glad I didn't.

Now my only connection to him is this story and a lifetime of aches and pain, to this day.

~

Afterword

by Susan Rukeyser, Publisher

Some folks have strong feelings about the "right" way to talk about abortion. Some think we should recount our experiences as if confessing secrets, with respect for what is obviously a "sensitive" topic, possibly offensive to others. *Don't tell the truth if it makes them uncomfortable*, is the message we receive from girlhood. Don't share too much about our often inconvenient, often bloody biology. But the common experiences of unwanted pregnancies, infertility, miscarriage, motherhood, and abortion: What if we just told the truth, without apology?

My first encounter with Bonnie's stories was a couple of years ago, in a cozy, private writing class here in the California high desert. Over coffee and organic snacks, a couple of sweet dogs curled in the corners, Bonnie opened her notebook and began reading her succinct accounts of abortion, before and after Roe v. Wade. I was immediately taken by her straightforward style. "And that was that" became a blunt yet meaningful refrain. Bonnie resists much introspection, allowing her experiences to speak for themselves. They were not unusual, but perhaps her honesty is. She always understood the connection between a woman's bodily autonomy and her freedom—and her safety. Bonnie did not doubt her ability to make her own decisions. She does not apologize for them now.

25

I told Bonnie her stories must be heard. I share her deep concern about the myriad ways Roe has been chipped away in recent years, to the point that, for many American women—especially poor women—abortion is already out of reach. Again. When Amy Coney Barrett was appointed to the U.S. Supreme Court, Bonnie decided to share her stories, despite whatever strong feelings some folks might have. I'm proud to help her bring them out of that cozy, private room and into the world. By helping to destigmatize what is actually quite ordinary, perhaps we can halt the further erosion of our rights.

What if we all just told the truth? Maybe, then, telling it would not take such bravery.

Author's Acknowledgements

By the very nature of my story, there are few witnesses to acknowledge and thank. My mother, of course, who shepherded me through my pre-Roe v. Wade experiences—with resolve and bravery—and my dad, silent but supportive in the background.

In 1970s Los Angeles, as a single mother trying to make my way out of deeply damaged self-esteem, I found an organization of feminist single mothers called "Momma". They were the support group I needed at the time, and if any of them are still out there, thank you.

And thank you to the health care community and women's movement who learned how to bring abortion care out of the shadows and back alleys, saving many desperate women's lives in the process.

Many years after putting these experiences behind me, I became motivated to write pieces of my lifetime of memories. Thanks to a writing class in Joshua Tree, I was given a safe platform to tell my story. I was encouraged by the openness of the group and guidance of more experienced writers.

I was also encouraged in my writing by Cholla Needles Arts & Literary Library, and by the Desert Split Open Mic, hosted by Susan Rukeyser.

www.ingramcontent.com/pod-product-compliance
Lightning Source LLC
Chambersburg PA
CBHW070050040426
42331CB00034B/2961